D1543737

YA
PN
1995.9
.P7
S35
1989

## DATE DUE

| DATE DUE | | | |
|---|---|---|---|
| DEC 1 0 2007 | | | |
| AUG 1 0 2009 | | | |
| | | | |
| | | | |
| | | | |
| | | | |
| | | | |
| | | | |
| | | | |
| | | | |
| | | | |
| AYLORD | | PRINTED IN U.S.A. | |

# MAKING

# M·O·V·I·E·S

# MAKING
# M·O·V·I·E·S

*by Perry Schwartz*

Lerner Publications Company
Minneapolis

*This book is dedicated to Carl Brookins and Richard Jamieson, without whose talent, teaching skills, and patience it could never have been written.*

## Acknowledgments

The photographs and illustrations in this book are reproduced through the courtesy of: David Boe, front cover, pp. 1, 10, 13, 34, 35, 36, 40, 42, 48, 51; Hollywood Book and Poster Co., pp. 2, 6, 39, 63, 64, back cover; Library of Congress, p. 9; Los Angeles Rams/photo by Greg Bell, p. 14; Collectors Bookstore, pp. 16, 33; Museum of Modern Art/Film Stills Archive, p. 18; Photofest, pp. 21, 24; Laura Westlund, pp. 23, 68; Seaver Center for Western History Research, Natural History Museum of Los Angeles County, p. 27; Wisconsin Center for Film and Theater Research, pp. 28, 60; Cleveland Public Library, p. 33, top left; Orion Pictures Corporation, p. 33, top right; Danny Chin/Star File, p. 46; California Raisin Advisory Board, p. 58; Cineplex Odeon Corporation, p. 66; Paul Wehrwein, p. 69; Allied Film & Video, pp. 74, 75, 76; LeeAnne Engfer, pp. 79, 80.

**The photograph on page 2 shows a scene from *Back to the Future* being filmed against a blue backdrop.**

LIBRARY OF CONGRESS CATALOGING-IN-PUBLICATION DATA

Schwartz, Perry.
  Making movies.

  Bibliography: p.
  Includes index.
  Summary: Describes what happens during the production of a motion picture and the jobs of all the people involved.
    1. Motion pictures—Production and direction—Juvenile literature. [1. Motion pictures—Production and direction] I. Title.
PN1995.9.P7S35   1989       791.43'023       89-12121
ISBN 0-8225-1635-7 (lib bdg.)

Manufactured in the United States of America

2  3  4  5  6  7  8  9  10  99  98  97  96  95  94  93  92  91  90

# Contents

Animated films, such as "The Flintstones," are just one of the many different kinds of movies.

# Introduction

In the United States, it's the movies. In Europe and Latin America, people call it cinema. In India, the world's largest feature film-producing nation, people call it *chalchitr*. In Hong Kong, which is known for the type of kung fu movies that made Bruce Lee famous, it's called *den inn*. In the Soviet Union, a country with a long and celebrated film history, it's referred to as *kinó*.

Wherever in the world there are people, there are movies. The universal appeal of the movies—light, shadows, and colors dancing on a silver screen—has made them one of the most powerful communication media ever devised.

Movies are more than *Star Wars*, *Rambo*, *Cinderella*, and *Robo Cop*. Movies, or **motion pictures**, come in many different forms and lengths, from an elaborate six-hour feature film made in India, to a simple five-minute home movie of your last birthday party.

When we think of "the movies," we may also think of

animated films, or cartoons. Animated films also vary in length, from a 30-minute television show like the "Jetsons" to a full-length film such as *Snow White and the Seven Dwarfs*. Some animated films are made with drawings. Others, like the "California Raisins," use real objects that appear to move by means of stop-motion photography, a process its creator, Will Vinton, called Claymation.

Motion pictures that feature real people and things are called **live action**, because the photographic subjects are real, or live. Live subjects are sometimes mixed with cartoon characters, as in *Who Framed Roger Rabbit?*

Some kinds of movies aren't called "movies." TV commercials, business films, and documentaries are types of movies, as are educational films and music videos.

The first motion pictures were made in 1888. Before then, no one had ever seen an image projected onto a screen. Projected images of a horse-drawn buggy crossing a bridge astonished everyone who viewed them. Some people thought they were magic; others thought they were the devil's work.

At first, filmmakers simply documented, or captured, everyday life around them. The titles of some of these early films tell what the movies were about: *Barbershop*, *The Kiss*, *Wrestling*, *Horse Shoeing*, and *Trapeze*.

Soon film pioneers in France, Great Britain, Russia, and the United States began experimenting with plot lines and "trick photography" to tell stories. The stories were often fairy tales, such as *Cinderella*, which was first made in 1899 by French filmmaker Georges Méliès.

Early movies did not include sound. Although audiences could see the actors' lips moving, they could not hear the actors' voices. From time to time, bits of dialogue appeared on the screen so the audience could follow the story.

This is what a movie camera looked like in 1896.

These "silent films," as they are called, were never really silent, but were shown with live musical accompaniment. Often it was just someone at a piano, but in many large theaters, full orchestras played. The first sound movies, or "talkies," complete with music, sound effects, and the actors' voices, began to be made in the late 1920s.

The movies have come a long way since their simple beginning. Many more movies are made now, about more subjects and for more reasons. Filmmakers still record life around us, but now they also show what life is like in space, on the moon, and deep under the ocean.

Movies—and their cousin, television—have become part of our everyday life. Motion pictures and television are now a multi-billion-dollar industry. They are produced in over 100 countries around the world. To serve this industry, a profession has developed that includes actors, directors, cinematographers, editors, producers, and other artisans.

In this book, you will learn about different kinds of motion pictures, about how movies are made, and about the many jobs required to make these movies.

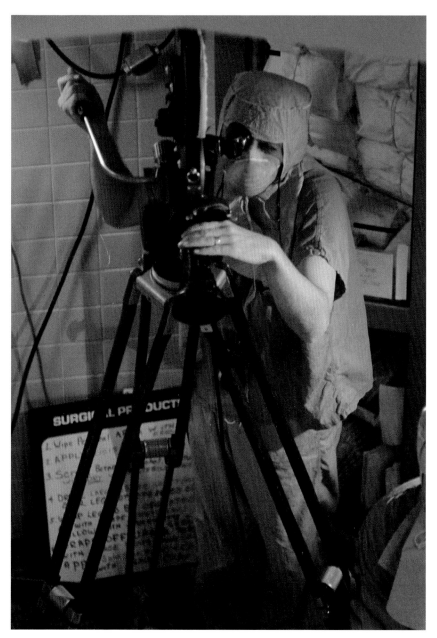

People make films to communicate ideas and information. A doctor might make a movie to demonstrate a medical procedure.

# Why People Make Movies

eople make movies to communicate ideas. These people have ideas they want to share, a story to tell. Movies are an effective way to communicate—especially feelings.

Printed communication, such as billboards or magazines, can offer only pictures and words. Radio offers only sound. Neither offers motion. Only the movies and television combine all three. The combination can be very powerful!

Some people think that the movies are the strongest communication tool ever invented. Francis Coppola, the director of *The Godfather*, *Apocalypse Now*, and *Tucker*, believes that "film is the most powerful medium of entertainment and intellectual expression in modern culture."

Often the information or ideas to be communicated are not those of the filmmaker. He or she is an artist who makes someone else's ideas visible. This is true whether the movie is a feature film, a business film, a sports training film, or a TV commercial.

Filmmakers can help present all kinds of information. Films can help a soup company sell a new kind of soup or help doctors and nurses learn a new medical procedure. The "information" may even be emotions, like the feelings we get when watching a music video.

## The Many Different Kinds of Movies

Here's a list of just some of the many different types of movies that are made.

| | | |
|---|---|---|
| Feature films | Music videos | Animated films |
| TV commercials | Training films | Industrial films |
| Medical films | Cooking films | Exercise videos |
| Sports films | TV programs | News films |
| Safety films | Travelogues | Documentaries |

There is not enough space in this book to discuss each of these kinds of film. What is important to know is that there are so many! While they all have something in common—each tells a story—each kind of movie listed above differs slightly from the others.

For example, a TV commercial must tell a story in 15, 30, or 60 seconds. The filmmaker and the advertiser must establish the theme of the commercial, identify the characters, and show the product in just a few seconds.

Most feature films, on the other hand, tell their stories in anywhere from 85 minutes to 3 hours or longer. Since the filmmakers have plenty of time to tell the main story, they can turn their attention to other considerations, such as developing the characters, action sequences, special effects, music, and special camera movements.

A sports film must also tell its story clearly, with lots of the kind of action that will please the sport's fans. The

A film about farming might be made by an agricultural company to show its products, or as an educational film.

people who make a film about a particular sport must know something about the sport itself as well as how to make movies. To succeed, the film should reflect the spirit of the sport and show what the audience expects to see.

A football audience wants to see scenes of the entire field to know what plays the teams have established, for example. But the audience also wants to see very close scenes of football players knocking into each other. The viewers also like to hear the sounds the football players make when they tackle each other.

A tennis audience wants to see the entire court. But unlike the football audience, the tennis audience isn't as interested in close-up scenes of the players. The tennis audience prefers to see how each player serves and returns the ball, how it is hit, and where it lands.

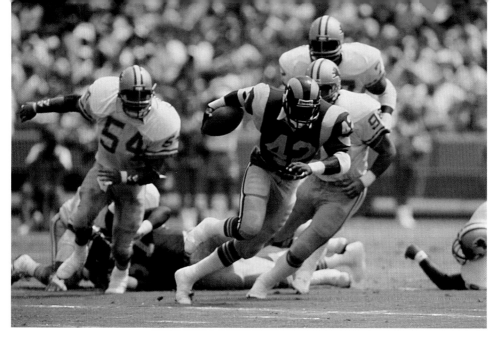

An audience watching a film about football expects to see close-up shots of the action.

The mood of these two sports is obviously very different. A successful film about each sport will convey the sport's mood while clearly showing what is happening. At the same time, the filmmaker must make sure that the film is being photographed properly, the sound is being recorded properly, and that dozens of other things are going well. It's a big job—bigger than one person can do by him- or herself.

## People in the Movie Industry

Making a film requires the talents and efforts of many people. Unlike writing books and painting, which are usually done by one artist, filmmaking is a collaborative art that uses the skills of many people.

Many different people work on every film, whether it's an educational movie or a sports film, a feature film or a music video. Here is a long but incomplete list of the people and jobs needed to make films. You've probably never heard of most of these people, because they work behind the camera, away from the "glamour" of the bright lights and the attention of the media.

The next time you go to the movies or watch TV, look at the credits—the list of jobs and the people who performed them—that appear at the beginning or end of the show. Here are some of the jobs you may see listed:

## Creative Positions

| | | |
|---|---|---|
| Art Director | Title Designer | Director |
| Animation Director | Executive Producer | Set Designer |
| Writer | Music Director | Principal Actor |
| Film Editor | Producer | Cinematographer |

## Technical/Support Positions

| | | |
|---|---|---|
| Assistant Director | Assistant Producer | Camera Assistant |
| Carpenter | Catering Chef | Production Secretary |
| Computer Operator | Music Editor | Continuity Person |
| Dubber Loader | Special Effects | Dolly Pusher |
| Crane Operator | Technician | Greenskeeper |
| Colorist | Projectionist | Grip |
| Gaffer | Generator Operator | Sound Recordist |
| Inker/Painter | Transportation | Backgrounder |
| Lab Technician | Captain | Helicopter Pilot |
| Location Scout | In-Betweener | Boom Person |
| Makeup Artist | Animal Trainer | Property Master |
| Matte Artist | Clapper/Loader | Script Supervisor |
| Production Auditor | Wrangler | Wardrobe Master |
| Publicist | Set Painter | Consultant |
| Security Guard | Sound Mixer | Production |
| Story Analyst | Stills Person | Manager |
| Wardrobe Attendant | Stand-In | Musician |
| Extra | Mechanic | Stuntperson |
| Electrician | Studio Teacher | Lab Technician |

Director George Lucas (*second from left*) and his crew at work in the Tunisian desert during the filming of *Star Wars*.

The jobs in this list have been divided into two categories, creative and technical/support. The difference between the two is important, but both kinds of jobs are needed to make a movie.

When they work together, these people are called a crew, just like a pilot, copilot, and flight attendants together are called an airplane crew. For the production of a movie to go smoothly, each member of the crew must do his or her job well. Making movies is a team effort!

What kind of person is attracted to a job in the motion picture industry? Typically, people who work in the movies like to communicate information. They are curious people who are keenly aware of the world around them and like to share what they know with others.

Many people in the movies also like to work on "projects," rather than "9-to-5" kinds of jobs. Project work has a beginning, middle, and end. Sometimes, as in a TV commercial, filming may only last one day. In the case of a feature-length film, the filming alone could last 3 months, and the entire project could take 18 months or longer. When that project is finished, everyone goes on to another project.

Most filmmakers work for themselves rather than a company. They are asked to work on a project because they have previous experience or are interested in the subject matter of the project.

Photographer Eadweard Muybridge first succeeded in taking pictures of motion—a horse running—in the 1870s. He set up 24 cameras in a row, with strings stretched from the cameras across a race track. When the horse ran by, it broke the string and triggered the camera to take a picture. His motion studies continued with sequences like this.

# How
# Movies Move

**S**imply defined, motion pictures are still pictures projected one after another so rapidly that they appear to be moving.

That's right—movies don't move. They're

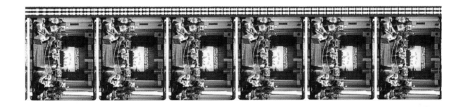

an illusion—the essence of magic! As you can see in the illustration, a strip of motion picture film is really a series of individual **frames,** or pictures. Each frame is a separate still picture. These still pictures are projected onto a movie screen so quickly that they appear to move.

You see the still images as moving because of persistence of vision. Your eye keeps seeing an image or picture for an instant after the image disappears. When movies are projected onto a screen, one image is separated from the next by a brief, dark interval. In between the projection of each still image or frame, a shutter in the movie projector blocks light from reaching the screen. A "light, dark, light, dark" pattern is created. During the dark interval, your eye retains the previous image even though it is now seeing the next image. The two images overlap and your brain melds them together to create the illusion of motion.

## The Motion Picture Camera

Individual still images are photographed onto motion picture film using a camera similar to a 35 mm still camera or 8 mm movie camera you might use to take pictures or home movies.

A motion picture camera differs from a consumer camera because it must move a roll of film along at an exact rate of speed. The camera's motor is usually set at a fixed rate to expose 24 frames of film per second. That is the rate set by filmmakers many years ago. They determined that at that rate the camera sees moving objects fluidly, or "normally." The camera motor turns a complex system of wheels, which advance the film through the camera.

Each frame of film comes to a part of the camera called the gate, where the camera's motor stops the film. The gate is like a window that opens to allow each frame of film to be exposed to light, which is focused by the lens.

Every camera has a lens, which functions as the camera's "eye." A motion picture camera lens is made of glass that has been ground and polished very carefully. If the glass

Joe Dante, who directed *Gremlins* and *The Burbs*, looks in the viewfinder of a motion picture camera. This kind of camera is commonly used to make feature films.

is not of the finest quality, the image might appear fuzzy or cloudy. The lens lets in and focuses the light that illuminates the subject to be filmed. The image formed by the lens is ready to be recorded onto film.

Behind the gate is a mechanical device called a shutter. The shutter, which looks something like an airplane propeller, passes in front of the gate. When the "propeller blade" is in front of the gate, it blocks the light. When it moves out of the way, light passes through to the film, and the camera takes a still photo of the image. Then the camera's motor advances the film to the next frame, and the procedure is repeated 24 times a second for movies filmed at normal speed. Some movie cameras designed to photograph at high speeds can expose up to 18,000 frames per second.

From a mechanical point of view, this is an extraordinary process, because the camera must hold the frame of film *absolutely* still while it is being exposed, or else the image will be blurry. At the same time, the film must remain flat against the gate. If the film ripples, parts of the image will be out of focus.

## Film

Film is to a filmmaker what canvas is to an artist. There are many different sizes and shapes of movie film, or **stock**: 8 mm, 16 mm, 35 mm, 65 mm, and 70 mm.

The size of motion picture film is always denoted in millimeters (mm). The size refers to the width of the film; 35 mm film means that the film is 35 millimeters wide. All still and movie film has holes on both outer edges. These holes are called sprocket holes and are used to guide the film through the camera.

## How Filmmakers Choose a Film Size

One reason film comes in so many different sizes is because filmmakers have wanted to project their movies onto bigger and bigger screens. Generally, the larger the film size is, the larger the image can be magnified and still remain bright and sharp.

In a typical motion picture theater, the screen onto which the image is projected is about 35 feet (12 meters) wide. Over the years, the technology used to make camera lenses and film stock has improved so much that it is now possible to project an image onto a screen as large as 90 feet wide by 70 feet high (25 x 20 m). That's wider than a nine-story building is high!

Filmmakers choose a film size based on a number of factors. Perhaps the most important question is where the movie will be shown, and how large the screen must be in order for the audience to see the movie. The budget (how much money the filmmaker has available to make the movie) may also determine which size film to use. Generally, smaller-sized film is less expensive to shoot. The smallest motion picture film size is 8 mm.

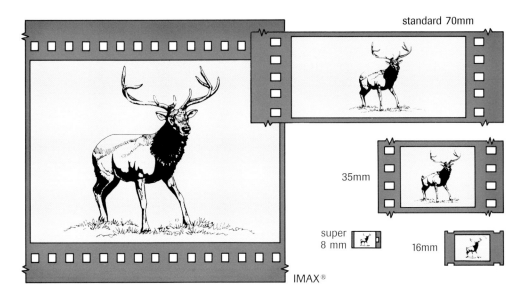

standard 70mm

35mm

super 8 mm

16mm

IMAX®

Movie camera film differs in size and shape.

No other sizes of motion picture film are available, but there are many, many different film **formats,** or shapes; these formats almost always use 35 mm or 70 mm film. The use of 70 mm film has spawned an area within the motion picture industry called specialty cinema. Feature films have not yet been made in any of these specialized formats — because it's very expensive to produce a feature-length film in 70 mm. But a wide variety of science, cultural, adventure, entertainment, and space films have been filmed in specialty cinema formats, such as IMAX® MagnaVision® ShowScan® and Super Cinema 3D®

William Friedkin directed *The French Connection* and *The Exorcist.*
Here he is working on *The Exorcist.*

# The People Who Make the Movies

S ome movies are made by only a few persons, while others require the talents of thousands. The size of the crew and the number of actors called for in the script depend on the kind of movie being made and the amount of money the producer—the chief executive of the movie—has budgeted to spend.

The producer, director, writer, cinematographer, and others in creative positions are the people primarily responsible for determining what the movie is going to be about and how the information or idea will be presented. They have the freedom to use their talents and do what they think is best, but they also have the responsibility of communicating a message to the audience effectively.

Without an audience, there is no reason for a movie— or painting, stage play, ballet, or song, for that matter— to exist. Successful filmmakers keep the needs of the audience in mind.

Here is an overview of some of the key jobs involved in making a feature-length motion picture.

## The Studio

The **studio** is not one person, of course, but is one of the large motion picture companies such as Warner Bros., Touchstone Pictures, United Artists, Twentieth Century Fox, Universal, Paramount Pictures, Tri-Star Pictures, and Orion Pictures. Since the early days of movies, though, the studio has often been thought of as a "person" because of the central role it played—and continues to play—in the making of feature-length motion pictures.

Years ago, studios financed, or paid for, and made most of their own movies. Often they made movies in large, fully equipped studios or soundstages (buildings designed to keep out unwanted noise during the shooting of a scene). The "studio" was the heart of the company, because that's where the company's product was made; the word *studio* was applied to the whole company.

In the United States, the first studios were in New Jersey, then New York and Chicago. Eventually, most of the studios moved to Los Angeles to take advantage of the warm, sunny weather. The first California studios set up shop in an isolated, rural neighborhood in Los Angeles called Hollywood. The rest is history.

Today, most of the theatrical movie industry is located *outside* of Hollywood in other parts of the Los Angeles area, but everyone still refers to Hollywood as the center of the U.S. motion picture business.

Most movies used to be made on studio sets. If a film called for a scene of New York City or a small Western town, the studio built entire blocks of buildings to look like New York streets or the main street of a Western town.

Hollywood has changed since the days when the studios first moved there. *Above*, Hollywood around 1900; *below*, panoramic view of Hollywood and Los Angeles today.

Early movies were filmed in studios. Here D.W. Griffith (in white hat, left) directs a scene from *Intolerance* in 1915.

Building these sets was cheaper than sending entire crews to remote locations. This kind of set is called a **standing set**, because it was left standing to be used over and over again for different movies.

At one time the studio controlled every aspect of filmmaking. Everyone who worked on the film, from the stars to the security guard at the front gate, worked for the studio. The studio was, in fact, a city within a city. There were cafeterias, barbershops, banks, drugstores, and other conveniences located right on the studio lot. Everything in the working life of a person in the movie business revolved around the studio.

Things have changed over the years. Today, the studio is mostly an office, although an important office. Many companies have sold off their back lots (the outdoor set areas). Contemporary movies are often filmed **on location**, which means filming in real places, with real streets, houses, and so on. The studio's primary function today is to finance a movie. The person who persuades a studio to pay for the production of a movie is the producer.

*The Producer*

Every movie begins with an idea. In the feature film part of the movie industry, that idea usually starts with the producer. The producer is responsible for finding an idea and "packaging" it—finding the right combination of stars, writer, and director that will make the movie attractive, or "saleable," to the studio.

The producer is always thinking about **story lines**, ideas that will make good movies. An idea for a movie can come from just about anything. To a producer, a good movie is one that the studio will "back," or support financially, and that the public will pay money to see. The idea may be original; that is, it occurred to the producer the way the words to a song occur to a songwriter. Or the idea may come from a book or stage play the producer has read or seen. It might also be an idea submitted to the producer by an agent, someone who represents a writer or book publisher.

Often the idea for a movie is taken from a movie that has already been successful. The producer hopes that another story featuring the same characters will also be popular. Because movies are so expensive to make, producers may avoid more risky, untried story lines in favor of a sequel, such as *Rambo II*, *The Empire Strikes Back*, or *Ghostbusters II*, which is based on characters with proven popularity.

Another important part of the producer's job is to determine the budget—how much money the movie will cost

—and control how that money is spent. A Hollywood movie can cost from $10 million to $45 million—or more.

Producers track the popularity of films in the **trades**, movie industry newspapers such as *Variety* and *The Hollywood Reporter*. The trades list the total amount of box office earnings, called **grosses**, for every major film playing in the United States, Canada, and certain foreign countries. Watching the current grosses helps the producer predict what audiences might want to see next year.

The initial idea for a movie can be very simple. For example, an idea might start out as "a movie about good and evil that takes place in the future, with a bad person who is out to control the universe, a handsome young man who is determined to crush the evil force, visits to planets with strange beings, intergalactic space fights, and plenty of special effects," and end up as *Star Wars.*

## The Screenwriter

The producer usually hires a writer to develop his or her idea into a **treatment**, which tells how the idea is to be treated, or presented, in the film. The treatment includes descriptions of the characters, sets, and action. The producer and the writer work together on the treatment. The writer knows what will make a good story on film, and the producer knows what sells at the box office.

The producer may know that a certain star actor, or **lead**, would like to play a particular kind of character. The producer will encourage the screenwriter to write such a part into the treatment so the producer can attract the star to the package. If the package contains the right elements—that is, the right stars, director, and story—the producer stands a very good chance of getting a studio to support the project financially.

Screenwriting is much different from writing for the page, such as a book, magazine article, or newspaper story. In addition to words, a screenwriter can take advantage of pictures, sound, and motion to help tell a story. Print writers often write for one person at a time—the reader of a book or newspaper, for example. A playwright or screenwriter, on the other hand, must write for groups of people.

Perhaps the most important difference is that the novel, newspaper story, or magazine article written by the writer is usually the final product. It may be edited or shortened to fit into a specific space, but what the writer writes is basically what you read.

A film script, however, is not the end, but the beginning of a movie. Before a movie is finished, the script, now called a **shooting script**, will be changed many times. Some scenes will be added, others cut. The producer might decide that he or she doesn't like a certain character and will "lobby," or work, to have it removed from the script. An actor may want to add personality traits that he or she feels will make the character better. The director may also feel the script needs changes made before it's ready to be filmed, such as different locations, different costumes, or more special effects.

One reason film is called a "plastic" medium is because the story—and how it is presented—can be molded, shaped, and constantly changed all the way through to the final editing.

## The Actors

Most feature films depend heavily on the lead characters to tell the story—and to sell the movie to the public. The lead characters are often played by stars.

If the producer and writer believe that a certain star is perfect for the role of the lead character, the producer will bargain or negotiate with the star's agent to see if the star will agree to be in the movie. Many factors enter into the negotiations, including: the type of role scripted for the star; how much the star will get paid; how many days of work will be required; and whether or not the star is working on another project when the producer plans to make the movie.

## The Director

The producer must also determine who the director of the movie will be. The choice of director is probably the most important decision the producer makes, because the director is the one person responsible for every creative aspect of the movie. The director is to a movie what a conductor is to a symphony orchestra—everyone follows his or her lead.

The director's skill lies in creating a vision of what he or she—or the client—wants to say on film. A good director knows how to use the skills of others, as well as filmmaking equipment, to help express that vision.

One part of the director's job is to decide how the script will be interpreted: Will it be funny or serious? How funny, or how serious? The director gets help from other people, but the director must be able to communicate his or her decisions to each person on the crew.

The director decides how the movie will look and "feel" to the audience. Will the film have a bright, happy sparkle to it, like *The Sound of Music*, or will it be dark and gritty, like *The French Connection*?

What mood should the cinematographer create with the lighting? What impression should the art director create

Four respected contemporary directors: *top left*, Francis Ford Coppola (*Apocalypse Now*, *Peggy Sue Got Married*); *top right*, John Sayles (*Eight Men Out*, *Baby It's You*); *bottom left*, George Lucas (*Star Wars*, *American Graffiti*); and *right*, Steven Spielberg (*E.T.*, *The Color Purple*).

An important part of a director's job is conferring with the actors about how they will play their roles.

with the sets and locations, and what feelings should be expressed in the music written by the music director? What kind of costumes work best? All these decisions are made by the director—with the help of the producer and other key creative people.

The most important part of the director's job is to help the actors interpret their characters. The director helps the actors to express the feelings of the characters in ways the audience will believe and accept. To do this job well, the director and the actors must know a lot about people and how people behave.

The director also chooses a cinematographer, art director, set designer, and music director. All of these people help the director turn his or her thoughts into reality on film.

All day, and perhaps all night, the director answers questions. "Should the couch be red or pink?" "Should

34

the actresses' hair be styled like this or like that?" "Do you want the camera to start back here and end up there, or the other way around?" "Is the light supposed to make the star look friendly or mean?" "It's getting close to lunchtime, do you want to stop now or shoot another scene?"

Everyone looks to the director for the answer, and only the director can give the answer. If he or she is right, the film may be a success. If he or she is wrong, the film could flop. A lot of money and careers ride on the decisions made by the director.

## The Cinematographer and Lighting Crew

The cinematographer, often called the director of photography or DP, determines how a scene is going to be lit to

The cinematographer creates a mood with lighting. Lighting can give the film many different looks, from eerie to bright.

The gaffer places a light where the cinematographer instructs him to.

best capture the mood the director wants. The cinematographer uses light to create a mood the way a visual artist uses paint.

The cinematographer relies on the **gaffer**, a lighting technician, to put the lights in place, and on the electrician to hook them up to an electrical source. Without the gaffer and electrician, the cinematographer and director couldn't do their jobs.

## The Costume Designer and Assistants

To determine what costumes are right for the movie, the director calls on the help of the costume designer, an expert in clothing design and fabric. If the movie is a **period story** (one that takes place in a period of time other than the present), the costume designer studies books, paintings, and drawings to find out what type of clothes were worn during that period. If the story occurs in the future, the costume designer can use his or her imagination to create almost any kind of costumes.

During the shooting of the film, the wardrobe master makes sure that each actor has his or her costume and that it is cleaned, pressed, and ready to wear.

## The Stuntpeople

Stunts are tricks that are usually performed by trained stuntmen and stuntwomen who perform the stunt instead of the star. A scene of a person falling off a horse or roof is performed by a stuntperson. Car chases are always performed by stuntpeople. Stuntpeople are used because the producer and director don't want to take the chance of the star being hurt. Or the star might not know how to ride a horse or fly a plane, for example, so the stuntperson stands in for the actor. Stunts can be dangerous, even for stunt experts, who practice the stunt many times before performing in front of the camera.

## The Technical/Support Crew

Most people in technical/support positions work on the movie only during the filming. These people help the creative people bring ideas to life. During the shooting of a scene, the director must watch and listen to the actors to make sure they are interpreting their roles well. If the director also had to move the camera, record the sound, or keep notes on which shots were good, he or she couldn't pay attention to the actors' performances. So the director needs the help of an assistant director, a dolly pusher, a sound recordist, and a script supervisor.

## The Assistant Director

The assistant director works closely with the director on the administrative aspects of the production. The "A/D," as he or she is called, organizes many details of the production. Along with the location scout, the A/D selects locations for the movie to be shot and suggests a shooting schedule, which tells the crew when and where each scene will be filmed. He or she also works with the production manager to determine budgets for various parts of the production, such as how much money it will cost to feed the crew and actors. The A/D also sets the call time, the time when the crew and actors are required to report for work each day.

During **principal photography**, which is the period when the main scenes of the film are photographed, the A/D assists the director in any way possible. The A/D also directs the background action on the set—the people you see walking on the sidewalk or in hallways behind the main action.

## The Dolly Pusher

The dolly pusher pushes a movable camera platform, called a **dolly**, as the actors walk. The dolly pusher must not walk too fast or too slow, but at exactly the same speed as the actors. It takes a person with special skill to push a dolly smoothly so the audience is not aware that the camera is moving.

If the sidewalk were bumpy, the camera would shake every time it hit a bump. That would be distracting to the

To film this scene in *Raiders of the Lost Ark*, dolly track is laid on the ground. The camera is mounted on the track, ready to roll. A stuntman for Harrison Ford, the star of the film, is in the background.

audience, so the director asks the help of other assistants and carpenters to lay down special rails, called dolly track, for the camera dolly to ride. These rails are similar to railroad tracks and help to smooth out the ride for the camera and the audience.

## The Sound Recordist and Assistants

The sound recordist, often called the mixer, is responsible for the quality of the sound recorded during the

A sound recordist gets his tape recorder ready to record the live sound of the scene being filmed.

shooting of a scene. This person usually operates the tape recorder and is often helped by the boom person, who operates the microphone (which is attached to a long pole called a "boom"). For musical films, the playback person operates a tape recorder with prerecorded music so the singers and dancers can adjust their movements to match the beat of the sound track music.

## The Script Supervisor

The script supervisor keeps **script notes**, a detailed record of the day's shooting. The notes contain comments by the director, such as which **take**, or attempt to shoot a scene, was preferred, and anything else that may help put the movie together later.

The script supervisor is also responsible for maintaining **continuity**, which means assuring that the action will match from one scene of the movie to the next scene. Scenes of a film are often photographed out of sequence, or the crew may break for lunch in the middle of shooting a scene. When the A/D calls "lunch," work stops—and everyone leaves the set. When shooting starts again, the script supervisor must remember what the set looked like and where everyone was.

The script supervisor watches each take closely and writes *accurate* notes—some people take instant photographs—to help remember details such as where the actors were standing, which hand an actor may have had in a pocket, and which pocket.

## The Production Assistant

The production assistant does whatever else is left to do. That may mean running last-minute errands, picking up meals for the cast and crew, or answering the telephone. In general, the "P/A" assists in any way possible. Small projects may have only one P/A, whereas a feature film may use many P/As.

The cinematographer prepares to film a scene of two fencers.

# Behind the Scenes During Filming

The beginning of filming is an exciting and anxious time for everyone associated with the production. After perhaps many years, the producer is finally realizing a dream of seeing his or her idea brought to the "silver screen" and the chance of having it witnessed by the public.

Plans and preparations for the filming, which is called the **shoot**, have been underway for months. Now, at last, and for the next two to four months, a group of people with specialized skills has come together to begin working as a crew.

The director has spent months preparing for the shoot. The production manager and assistant director have revised budgets and schedules 10 times or more, but now they are locked in. The actors have memorized their lines and studied the characters they're going to portray. The costume designer has added the final touches to the costumes.

The director of photography has made camera tests to check the lighting and assure that the equipment is working. The sound recordist has assembled the proper microphones to record the sound. The wardrobe people have fitted the actors with the costumes and made last-minute adjustments to hems and sleeve lengths.

The makeup people have tested the actors' makeup under the hot lights to make sure it looks right. The set designer and carpenters have built the sets. The prop people have found just the right furniture, rugs, and paintings for the rooms. The special effects team and the stunt crew have practiced and perfected their stunts. If there are child actors, the teacher has set up a portable schoolhouse for them to study in, between scenes. The "chuck wagon" has been set up nearby, and the chef is preparing lunch for the cast and crew.

All of this has been done according to the director's instructions—and, so far at least, within the producer's budget. Now, at last, shooting begins.

## Lights! Camera! Action!

Few, if any, directors actually yell the famous words "Lights! Camera! Action!" But when the cameras begin to roll, a movie is being made. It is a special time for the people involved, one that is unmatched in almost any other profession.

What happens behind the scenes when a film is being made? Imagine that the following scene is going to be shot on a studio back lot:

A male and female lead are driving a car down a street. Suddenly they hit an explosive charge, and their car veers wildly into the opposite lane, causing an oncoming car to leap up onto the curb and strike a fire hydrant. The broken hydrant shoots out a stream of water, which attracts the attention of the neighborhood dogs. They all start barking their displeasure at losing a favorite landmark. The first car jumps the curb on the other side of the street, striking a pedestrian. The pedestrian holds on as best he can as the car continues wildly down the sidewalk and then back onto the street. Finally the car strikes a tree, throwing the pedestrian into a hammock. The male lead looks out the window to see where the pedestrian landed, and a bird's nest lands right on top of his head. As he removes it, an egg falls, breaking on his head. He finishes the scene with a look of disgust.

You can probably tell by the treatment of this scene that it is a comedy. If you were watching the action on the set during filming, you would see periods of intense commotion, as well as times of inactivity. Here is what might happen as the scene is being filmed.

By checking the call sheet, crew members know exactly when the first crew call of the day is scheduled. Much of the work probably starts early in the morning, very early, around 5:00 A.M., when the actors begin their makeup sessions. Other crew members have different call times, depending on how long they think it will take them to prepare to shoot the scene.

The call times are based on what time of day the director wants to shoot the scene. The director has consulted with the cinematographer, who has told the director that it would be best to shoot the scene before the sun gets high in the sky. If the sun is too high, it will cast unpleasant shadows on the actors' faces.

The director then called a meeting with other key people on the crew and asked them how long it would take them

Even Miss Piggy has makeup and wardrobe attendants to get her ready for a shoot.

to prepare their work. Based on that discussion, the assistant director wrote up the day's call sheet and posted it where everyone could see it.

Most movie stars only have to get themselves from their home or hotel to the studio's front gate. Because studios are so big, actors could drive around for hours looking for the set they are supposed to be on. So the assistant director has arranged with the transportation captain to have limousine drivers meet each star at the front gate and drive them to the set or soundstage.

The actors are dropped off at a special trailer marked "Makeup." Important actors—big stars like Meryl Streep or Tom Cruise—have their own trailers, which give them a private place to rest and study their lines between scenes.

These actors are also assigned their own makeup and wardrobe attendants.

Meanwhile, the camera crew is preparing the camera equipment. The cinematographer is judging the quality of the sunlight and working with the gaffers to place extra lights along the street where the scene is to be filmed. The lights must not be seen by the camera, so the **best boy**—the chief gaffer—instructs his crew to place the lights carefully.

To check the lighting that will fall on the actors, the cinematographer asks the **stand-ins**, people who look similar to the actors playing in the scene, to stand in place while the lights are adjusted. This saves time by allowing the crew to light the scene while the actors are having their makeup applied and wardrobe fitted. It also saves the actors from having to stand under the hot lights for long periods of time, which can tire an actor and ruin the makeup.

The first assistant camera operator is placing the camera on the camera car, a special vehicle that allows the camera to travel along with the car that is being filmed. The second assistant camera operator is loading unexposed film into magazines. Magazines are light-tight chambers that hold film and are detachable from the camera. If the movie is being shot in 35 mm film, each 1000-foot (300 m) load of film will last about 10 minutes. Twenty to thirty magazines will be loaded at a time to minimize the wait when the assistant changes the film in the camera.

Often the second camera assistant is called the clapper/loader because, in addition to loading film magazines, he or she also operates the **clap slate**, a chalkboard used to help synchronize the picture with the sound. When the film editor sees the arm of the slate touch the slate, he stops

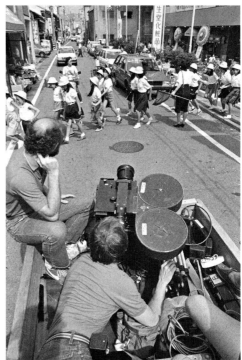

*Top left*: A crew member loads film into the camera. To the left of the camera is the magazine, which holds more film. *Top right*: The director, cinematographer, and other crew members ride in a camera car to film the street scene behind them. *Left*: The clap slate shows information about the film being made; in this case, the film is called *Faces of Japan* and the slate shows that the crew is filming the first take of the scene.

the picture. When he hears the first sound (or "clap") made by the arm as it strikes the slate, he stops the sound. The clap slate also gives information about the film, such as the title and the take number.

The sound crew is preparing the boom microphone to record the actors' voices and the sounds of the cars as they drive down the street. Usually a cable is used to get the sound to the tape recorder. But the mixer may choose to use a wireless microphone instead. A wireless microphone uses a radio transmitter rather than a cable. The transmitter is about the size of a portable tape player and is hidden from the camera's view either in the actor's back pocket or in the small of his or her back. The microphone is tiny, about the size of a peanut, and can be concealed easily behind a tie or shirt collar or inside a blouse or dress.

Over to the side, the special effects team is preparing a special breakaway fire hydrant that will snap apart easily when struck by the car. Working with plumbers, they have connected a huge hose to the inside of the fake hydrant. On cue, when the car hits the hydrant, a stream of water will gush through the hose and out of the broken hydrant.

The assistant director is walking along the street with another group of special effects people, talking about where to place the explosive charge that will blow the tire. The special effects technicians need to know what the camera will see as it moves down the street so they can hide the wires connecting the charge to a battery. They agree on a spot to put the charge, and the special effects team begins its work. Safety issues are also discussed, and plans are made to have a fire truck and ambulance standing by in case of an emergency.

Behind a house, in a portable kennel, animal trainers are practicing with 50 dogs of various breeds, using an exact replica of the fire hydrant on the street. All the dogs have been trained to work in the movies. The trainers use special commands to get the dogs to respond just as the script requires. Of course, the dogs get special treats when they do their job right.

Not far away, the stuntpeople are rehearsing their part of the scene. A stuntman, specially trained to do dangerous stunts, is jumping onto the hood of a slow-moving car. Because he is the same height and build as the actor, the stuntman has been chosen to stand in for the actor who plays the pedestrian. The wardrobe department will dress the stuntman in a suit and tie similar to those the actor wears. The camera will show a wide shot of the action — so wide that the audience will not be able to tell that the stuntman is not the same person as the actor.

Another group of stuntpeople, who are experts in special, or trick, driving, walk along the street where the scene will be shot. They refer to the planning sheet they made weeks ago that describes how many kinds of car collisions the director wants to show and where they occur. Next they run a safety check on the cars they're going to use.

From the outside, these cars look like any standard automobile. Inside, they're very different. The frame of each car has been reinforced with steel to protect the driver during the collision. The windows are made of shatterproof glass. Inside is a host of safety devices to protect the driver from injury in case something goes wrong.

Not far away, the **grips**, people who carry the equipment around a movie set, are putting another car — which is just like the leads' car — onto a special platform trailer. The platform trailer is used to film close-up shots of the actors in the car. The trailer, 30 feet (9 m) long and 15 feet

A grip carries equipment around the movie set or location.

(4.5 m) wide, is a flat platform only about 6 inches (15 centimeters) off the ground. There is room on the trailer for the car, the camera, the camera crew, and the lights. When the camera is focused on the actors talking, the audience can't tell that the driver is *not* actually driving the car. Because the actor doesn't have to think about driving, he can concentrate on acting. And the camera operator knows that the car will always be where it's supposed to be.

The greenskeepers, who are responsible for the trees, grass, plants, and shrubs on a set, are working with the set builders and carpenters to construct a special "tree" for the hero's car to crash into. (Of course, a stunt driver will be driving the car when the crash occurs.) The property people, meanwhile, are busy up in the tree, readying the bird's nest—and a couple of dozen eggs—that will fall on the hero's head.

The actors are finished being made up and are now in the wardrobe trailer, where they are being fitted with their costumes. The producer is meeting with the production accountants in an office the studio has given him to use during the shooting.

Close by, another film crew is interviewing the director as part of a "behind-the-scenes" feature for a cable TV show. A production assistant helps the film crew move around the set without getting in the way. On this day, too, one of the stars' agents has decided to watch the filming, so a production assistant is finding a director's chair for him. The security guard has set up a barrier to let other people on the back lot know that filming is going to occur.

The assistant director is looking at her watch, concerned that the director at least gets started on filming before the crew stops work for the morning break. Using a walkie-talkie, the A/D confers with her assistants to determine if all the preparations have been made and everyone is ready.

The director and the actors have rehearsed the scene together, and it's been agreed how each actor is going to interpret his or her role. Now comes the time when the director and actors must do the scene in front of the camera. The crew has already done a run-through of the scene, practicing each element of the scene before shooting begins.

Shooting a scene of a movie requires the best work of everyone on the crew. The more complicated the scene, the more difficult it is for that to happen. If one person makes a mistake, if an actor forgets his lines, if one piece of equipment fails, or if one simple effect doesn't work, the entire scene must be reshot.

Many takes of the scene may be shot before the director is satisfied. When the director is finally happy that he has the best performance from everyone on the set, he yells "Print it!" That's the signal that this scene is over and everyone can move on to the next setup.

The stuntpeople playing the actors now take their starting positions inside the car. (The real actors will be used later, for the close-up shots.) The camera car, which looks like a pickup truck, is moved into place. At the back of the camera car is a crane, or movable arm, on which the camera is mounted. The crane can move up and down and to the left and right.

For this scene, the director wants the camera to start close to the car and at the same height as the car door. Then, just before the tire blows, the camera will "crane up" high in the air so the audience can see the out-of-control movements the car makes.

"Light 'em up!" yells the best boy. The lights along the street are turned on. The cinematographer checks the lighting on the stuntpeople, making any necessary changes. He also measures with a **light meter** the amount of light falling on the stuntpeople. The assistant sets the f-stop on the camera's lens based on the light meter reading. The f-stop adjusts the size of the opening through which light enters the lens. If the setting is incorrect, the picture could be underexposed (too dark), or overexposed (too bright).

Then the first assistant camera operator carefully sets the lens to the proper focus. If this is not done properly, the picture will be blurry.

The assistant sound mixer now conceals the wireless microphones and transmitters on the actors. The sound mixer then asks each actor for a level, which means the actor must speak a few words so that the recording volume can be set properly.

The camera operator looks through the viewfinder of the camera and sees exactly the picture that will be photographed on film. He asks the crane operator to adjust the height of the crane so he can see into the car better.

The director climbs on board the camera car and takes his special chair next to the camera so he can observe the action. "I'm ready," he says. "Let's shoot it."

"Stand by!" yells the assistant director. "Quiet on the set!" Using the walkie-talkie, she notifies all the other people involved in the scene that the director is ready to begin.

The sound mixer pushes a button that makes a loud buzzing noise. It's very harsh, and it tells everyone within listening range that shooting is about to begin. "Start the car," the assistant director tells the stuntman behind the wheel. "Ready, everyone?" asks the director.

"Wait a minute," says the stuntman playing the actor from behind the wheel. "You better put the camera farther away from me. I'm afraid I might hit the camera car when the tire blows."

"But that will make the picture too wide," says the director. "The lights will be in the shot."

"I can put another lens on the camera," says the cinematographer. "That will allow the camera to move farther away from the car and still get the same size picture." "OK," says the director, "do it."

The assistant camera operator searches through the box of lenses for the right lens. It takes a couple of minutes to replace the lens, recheck the focus distance with the tape measure, and set the f-stop, but now the shooting is ready to start again.

"All right, everyone. Let's go," says the director. Once

again the sound mixer pushes the button that makes a loud buzzing noise. "Roll sound," says the assistant director. The sound mixer starts the tape recorder. The clapper/loader stands in front of the camera.

"Camera," shouts the director. The camera operator looks into the viewfinder. The assistant camera operator pushes a button to start the camera's motor. "Speed," says the sound mixer, acknowledging that the motors of the camera and the tape recorder are working properly. "*Donovan: Private Eye.* Scene 401. Take 1. Sound take 1," says the clapper/loader. Then he raises the arm of the clap slate and drops it down onto the slate with a loud "snap." "Action," yells the director.

The camera car starts off, followed by the car with the stuntpeople playing the actors in it. The car gets to the place where the explosive charge is supposed to be detonated — but nothing happens. "Cut," says the director. Everything and everyone stops. "Cool 'em off," yells the best boy, and the gaffer throws a switch to shut off the lights.

The special effects team runs over to the scene. They check all their electrical connections and decide to replace the charge. "Sorry," one man says to the director. "This one should work."

"OK, let's try it again," says the director. Everyone goes back to their starting positions. "Light 'em up!" shouts the best boy again. Quickly, everything is rechecked. The A/D is looking at her watch — only five minutes to go before the cast and crew are supposed to have their break.

The sound mixer pushes the button that makes the loud buzzing noise. "Roll sound," says the assistant director again. The sound mixer starts the tape recorder again. The clapper/loader stands in front of the camera.

"Camera," shouts the director, and the camera operator again looks into the viewfinder. The assistant camera operator starts the camera. "Speed," says the sound mixer. "*Donovan: Private Eye.* Scene 401. Take 2. Sound take 2," the clapper/loader says. Then he drops the arm of the clap slate onto the slate with another loud "snap." "Action," yells the director.

The camera car starts off again, followed by the actor's car, driven by the stuntman. At a prearranged point, the assistant director cues the oncoming car to start toward the actor's car. The hero's car hits the mark on the road and the special effects person throws the switch that explodes the charge. It works! The car's tire blows with a big bang.

The A/D cues the stunt driver in the opposite car to move forward. The stuntman who plays the hero drives his car out of control, veering it into the opposite lane. To avoid crashing into the hero's car, the stunt driver in the oncoming car jumps the curb and strikes a fire hydrant.

At the moment of impact, the plumbers turn a valve and water shoots into the air. The animal trainers cue the dogs, and all 50 dogs run into the street barking. They surround the car and the hydrant.

The A/D cues the stuntman playing the pedestrian to start walking down the sidewalk. The leads' car jumps the curb and, from the camera's point of view, appears to hit the man. Actually, the stuntman leaped onto the hood of the car at the last minute, but the audience can't see the trick.

As the pedestrian stuntman rolls across the hood of the car and grabs onto the windshield, the driver stops the car. This is as much of the scene as they will do now.

The rest of the scene will be filmed using the car on the platform trailer—and the real actors playing their parts.

"Cut," yells the director. "That was great. How was it for you?" he asks the camera operator. "Great," he replies. "How was it for sound?" the director asks. "Good," says the mixer.

"Print it!" shouts the director. "We'll do the close-ups after break." "Rest period," the A/D says into a bullhorn so everyone can hear. "Thirty minutes. Everyone assemble at the far end of the street when the break is over." The cast and crew head over to the chuck wagon for coffee, juice, tea, and rolls.

Shooting just one part of this scene took three hours. Though exciting, the process is tedious and time-consuming. On a good day—which is 10 hours long—only about one and one-half minutes of actual screen time is filmed.

## The Wrap

At the end of principal photography, when the last take of the last scene has been filmed and is "in the can," the A/D yells, "That's a wrap!" This means that filming is finished and everything can be wrapped up and put away—until the next project. Often the entire cast and crew gather for a "wrap party" to celebrate the end of filming and wish everyone good luck in the future.

Wrapping a film is a special time, because the cast and crew have worked closely with each other and have become dependent on one another for a short but intense period of time. These people may not work together again, but friendships have been made that can last a lifetime.

The "California Raisins" TV commercials are made using stop-motion photography in a style of animation called Claymation.

# Special Effects and Animation

**S**pecial effects are those dazzling, spectacular techniques that made the shark in *Jaws* appear to eat Quint, King Kong seem to climb the Empire State Building, and the train crash through the "train station" in *Silver Streak.*

When the film script calls for a scene that is difficult or impossible to photograph in real life, the director turns to the special effects director and his or her team of "movie magicians." Their job is to create the special effects that will make illusions pass for real life.

The special effects team uses many tricks to make you believe an illusion, but every special effect comes from one or more of three basic motion picture principles. The first is the same one that film animation relies on, the principle that film does not have to be photographed continuously. Exposing one frame of film at a time is called **stop-motion photography**.

Using stop-motion photography, special effects people

made the walkers in *The Empire Strikes Back* appear to be walking across the moon. After the special effects team shot one frame of film, someone moved each walker's legs to a new position. Then another frame of film showing the new position was exposed, and so on, until the entire sequence was photographed. When the sequence is projected, the walkers seem to move because of persistence of vision.

Another principle the special effects team relies on is that of illusion. Models, miniatures, drawings, and masks are created and filmed to make them appear full-sized. The King Kong that climbed the World Trade Center in the 1976 remake was only 40 feet (12 m) high—and he was made out of Styrofoam!

The gorilla that held Jessica Lange captive in *King Kong* was made of Styrofoam.

The third special effects principle is **composite photography**, which means combining separately photographed images onto one strip of film. The Styrofoam model of King Kong was photographed climbing a miniature of a World Trade Center tower. Then the real World Trade Center towers were photographed with people standing on the street looking up at the building as if King Kong were really there. In the laboratory, these two separate pieces of film were combined, so it appears that King Kong is climbing a real tower and real people are watching him.

## Stunts As Special Effects

Stunts are another area of special effects. One of the most famous uses of stunts for a special effect was in the 1966 auto racing film *Grand Prix*. The director wanted to show a number of race cars crashing. The director hoped to film the crashes from several different angles.

The situation posed a problem. When race cars are traveling at over 100 miles (160 kilometers) per hour, the drivers have little control over the cars' behavior, so there was no guarantee that the cars would crash where the director wanted them to. To solve the problem, the special effects team devised a hydrogen cannon that shot race cars out like bullets. The cannons could be aimed exactly where the director wanted the cars to crash. Dummies dressed as drivers were used instead of real people, because the stunt was so dangerous.

Many movies rely on special effects to help tell their story. When an actor gets "shot" in the movies and you see "blood" coming from the wound, what you're really seeing are exploding capsules of stage blood, a liquid made to look like real blood. The capsules are fitted on top of explosive caps, which are connected by wires to a battery. When the explosive cap is set off by remote control, the cap opens a small hole in the clothing and causes the "blood" to gush out of the "wound." When the special effects team connects all the wires for the "bullet hits" to an actor, it looks like a plate of spaghetti is stuck to the actor's body.

## Makeup As a Special Effect

For some movies, "makeup" means simply powders and creams that are applied to actors' faces to make them look good under the hot movie lights. But makeup can also be considered a special effect. If a young actor has to look very old, or if an actor must play a horrible-looking monster or werewolf, makeup artists create the required look.

Makeup can range from the wrinkles, sagging jaws, and baggy eyes that Marlon Brando wore as Don Vito Corleone in *The Godfather* to Linda Blair's scary revolving head in *The Exorcist*.

Sometimes it takes more than five hours for a team of makeup artists to make up an actor. Then the actor must work for 8 to 10 more hours in front of the camera. In *Planet of the Apes*, each ape mask weighed almost 50 pounds (23 kilograms). Needless to say, the actors really worked hard during the making of that movie.

Most masks, such as the one worn by Eric Stoltz, who played Terry in *Mask*, are made from latex, a type of rubber that molds to the face of the actor.

## Animation

Probably the most well-known and common form of animation is **cel animation**. Mickey Mouse, the Jetsons, Roger Rabbit, and Bullwinkle are examples of this type

Eric Stoltz's mask in the movie *Mask* was made of latex, a kind of rubber that can be molded to an actor's face.

Roger Rabbit came to life partly because of computer animation.

of animation. It is called cel animation because drawings are made onto sheets, or "cels," of clear acetate (a kind of plastic).

Using the principle of stop-motion photography, an artist draws a slightly different picture on each cel and then a camera operator photographs the cels one at a time on a special camera device called an animation stand. There are separate cels for the foreground and background. Just one frame may include 10 or more cels, one stacked on top of the other. Each one contains a small part of the entire scene. It takes a lot of cels to make an animated movie like *Pinocchio* or *Cinderella*, perhaps hundreds of thousands!

There are many other kinds of animation. "Gumby" is an example of a style of animation called **puppet animation**. The "California Raisins" TV commercials use a technique called **Claymation**. The process combines clay, which is what the characters are made of, with real props and sets. In claymation and puppet animation, the characters are moved a little bit at a time and photographed one frame at a time—each time in a new position or with a new expression.

The penguins' dance in *Mary Poppins* and the laser sword fight in *Star Wars* used **hands-on animation**. To create this kind of animation, artists add to what has already been photographed by drawing directly onto frames of film. These drawings are combined with other frames of film to create the illusion that cartoons and real-life characters are on-screen together.

Still other forms of animation have been developed with the advent of sophisticated computers. Computer animation was used in parts of *Who Framed Roger Rabbit?* and in the opening and closing scenes of "ABC's Wide World of Sports" and "CBS Tuesday Night at the Movies."

After a film has been shot, it begins the long journey to a movie theater.

# Finishing and Distributing the Movie

As each day's filming ends, the clapper/loader collects all of the exposed film and sends it to a laboratory for processing. The lab works all night to process the film so it will be ready for the director and crew to look at in the morning. Because the footage is ready to view the next day, it is called dailies.

When the director and crew have finished shooting the movie, the dailies, which are now called the **work print** (because what is worked with is a copy printed from the original film that went through the camera), and the sound recordings are given to the editor.

### The Film Editor

The editor is a person who connects together the hundreds of individual scenes that the director and the crew have photographed (which often amounts to hundreds of thousands of feet of film) to tell the story. The editor's job is very important, because how and when the scenes are joined together makes a great deal of difference to what the finished movie is like.

For example, say that the director photographed three scenes: one of a woman facing to the right and holding a gun; one of a train moving left to right; and one of a man looking to the left. The editor can connect these scenes in different ways. The illustration below shows two ways in which the separate scenes might be connected by the editor. The audience would draw a different conclusion from each sequence.

scene 1                              scene 2                           scene 3

scene 1                              scene 2                           scene 3

According to how an editor arranges these scenes, the audience will reach different conclusions. In the first sequence, the woman appears to be pointing a gun at the train, which is about to run over the man. In the second sequence, the train seems to be about to run over the woman, who is pointing the gun at a man.

The editor works at a machine that plays the dialogue and picture of each scene. He can make cuts on the splicing block.

The editor works at a machine that displays the picture and plays the sound of each scene. Using the machine, the editor determines where to cut, or splice, one scene to another. Then he or she tapes the pieces of film together on a device called a **splicing block**. The editor assembles the film—which in its final form is about 90 minutes long—from hours and hours of takes. Part of what the editor eliminates is unusable footage.

The director usually shoots—or "takes"—one scene many times. Sometimes the editor has only the one take that the director "printed." Other times, the editor looks and listens to many takes over and over to select the best take of each scene. He or she determines which is the best take, both technically and artistically. Among the factors the editor considers are: How good is the actor's performance in the take? Does the performance equal the performance in scenes that come before and after? Is the scene in focus? Is it properly exposed?

Sometimes the actor's performance is good, but part of the scene is out of focus. In this case, the editor will probably use just part of the scene. If the editor has no other acceptable takes of the scene, he or she will inform the director and the producer, who decide whether or not to reshoot the scene or eliminate the scene from the movie.

Reshooting is very expensive. When principal photography is finished, the sets and props are dismantled, returned, or destroyed, and the actors and crew leave the project to begin working on other films. It is impossible to substitute the star actors, and very hard to find look-alikes for the bit players, those actors with minor roles.

Eliminating the scene from the movie could change the story or make it confusing for the audience. Deciding what to do is difficult and may have expensive consequences. The producer must make the decision.

When the editor has finished screening all the footage and has selected the good takes, he or she begins to assemble the "selects" into the **first cut**, or version, of the movie. Now the editor's creative skill comes into play as each scene is viewed in relation to the scenes before and after it to determine if the order of the scenes is good and the cuts have been made in the right places, to tie the scenes together, and to set the pace and rhythm of the film.

At this point the editor is working only with the picture and dialogue. Once a sequence, or series of scenes, is put together, the editor will work with a sound effects editor—one of many editing assistants—to create the necessary sound effects.

## Creating Sound Effects

The sound effects editor examines each film sequence very carefully, noting all the possible sounds that could be a part of the scene. These could include sounds like a door opening, a dog barking, gunshots, thunder, or tires squealing.

When the sound effects editor has finished the list, he or she then has to find or create each effect. Often the effect exists, either from a previous film or in a special sound effects library. In this library, the editor can look up the category of "sirens," and find sound effects for many different kinds of sirens, such as "fire," "police," "air raid," "ship's general quarters," and so on.

If the sound effect doesn't exist, the sound effects editor must create it. Creativity, skill, and inventiveness are needed. For example, if the scene calls for the sounds

A sound recordist captures the sound of falling water at a Japanese temple. If he couldn't record the effect himself, he could probably find it at a sound effects library.

of a burning building, it would be difficult—and very expensive—to actually burn a building just to get the sound of the fire. So a sheet of cellophane is crinkled in front of a microphone to simulate the sound of fire.

After all the sound effects have been created, the editor places each one in sync (short for synchronization) with the picture so the sound will exactly match the picture. It's critical that the sound of a door opening be heard at the exact instant the door is opened, otherwise it would be "out-of-sync" and distracting to the audience.

As in real life, in movies many things happen at the same time. As the editor works to develop the sound effects for a sequence, he or she adds layer upon layer of sounds. The scene may show a dog barking while two actors are talking and a truck drives by. The editor must include the sounds for each of these parts of the picture.

## Rerecording Dialogue

Despite the elaborate preparations made during shooting, many feature films do not keep the sound of the actors' voices that was recorded on location. They use the recording as a guide for the actors to rerecord their dialogue in a sound booth. This is because some noise, like an airplane flying overhead, usually occurs during a take and compromises the quality of the sound.

In a technique known as **automatic dialogue replacement** (ADR), the actors look at a short scene of the film projected on a screen just outside the sound booth and speak their lines along with the film. The scene is projected using a projector that runs both forward and backward. The scene is run over and over until the actor speaking in the booth has exactly matched the mouth movements made during the filming of the scene. The new dialogue is given to the sound editor to lay in, or replace, with the original sound recording.

## Creating the Music

When the editor has assembled all the movie's sequences, the music director looks at the cut, talks with the director about the mood the music should impart, and begins to write a musical score. Then the music track is added to the dialogue track and the sound effects tracks.

Next the director and producer look at the final cut of the film and approve what the editor and his or her assistants have done. The film's sound track is now ready to be mixed, or blended.

## The Sound Recording Studio

The picture, the actors' dialogue, all the sound effects, and the music are brought to a recording studio where a rerecording engineer **mixes**, or blends, the various sounds together into the final sound track. The rerecording engineer places the music and sound effects on special machines called **dubbers**, which play all of the sounds in sync with the picture.

The film editor, director, and rerecording engineer look and listen to each sequence and mix all the sounds to the appropriate volume. Most of the time this means that the sound of the dog barking will be lower than the sound of the actors talking to each other. But for a special effect, say to scare the audience, the sound of the dog barking may grow louder than the actors' voices, creating a sense of fear in the audience.

## Creating Titles

Now that the sound track is finished, the title designer

creates the design for the credits, which appear at the beginning and end of the film. He or she selects a typeface and determines where and how in the picture the type will appear. After the director approves the design, the title designer photographs the titles on the animation stand. They are then added in the laboratory to the finished movie.

## The Film Laboratory

Now the work print and sound track of the movie go to the film laboratory to be finished. Until now, the edited film has been in two separate parts, the picture and the sound track. At the laboratory these two parts are copied

Strips of film are processed at film development laboratories like this one.

A technician operates a film printer.

onto one piece of film, which is what is eventually shown in the movie theater. But much work remains before the film is shown in the theater.

## Putting It All Together

At the lab, specially trained technicians called conformers, or negative matchers, match the scenes of the work print copy chosen by the editor with the corresponding scenes in the exposed negative film that passed through the camera. Conformers must be precise in their work and have a lot of patience. They have to look through thousands of feet of film to find the exact beginning and ending film frame that the editor has chosen for each scene in the movie.

Every strip of motion picture film has a series of numbers at the edge of the frame at one-foot intervals. The conformers use these numbers to match the work print scenes with the negative scenes.

Other technicians, called timers, begin their work when the conformer has assembled all the negative scenes of the movie. The timer's job is to "time," which means adjusting the color and brightness of each scene according to the requests of the director.

While the timers are working with miles of picture negative, still other technicians in the sound department of the lab are busy transferring, or copying, the sound track made at the recording studio to an optical negative.

Film negatives are timed electronically on this machine.

An **optical negative** is a photographic copy of the sound track.

If you hold a piece of movie film to the light, you'll see a tiny squiggly line at one edge of the film—that's the sound track. The movie projector changes the light energy of the optical sound track into sound energy, which is then played through the speakers in the theater.

**The sound track is visible on the strip of film as squiggly lines to the left of the frames.**

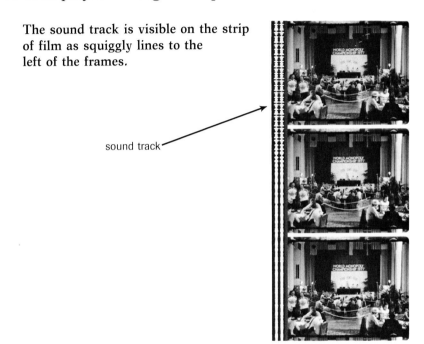

sound track

When the timer and the sound department staff have finished their jobs, the picture negative and the optical negative are given to the printing department. Technicians in this department print, or copy, the two negatives onto an unexposed length of film, which is then processed.

## *Viewing the Finished Film*
The very first print of the finished movie, with the

picture and sound on one piece of film, is called the **answer print**. Everyone who worked on the project is anxious to see it. The laboratory's customer service representative calls the producer to let him or her know that the answer print is ready to be screened, or viewed, in a small movie theater called a "screening room."

The producer, in turn, may call a representative of the studio, the director, the editor, and many of the stars and crew, and they all gather in a screening room to view the fruit of their labors. It is a very exciting time.

Sometimes the producer or studio want to test the public's reaction to the movie, so they schedule "sneak previews" and ask the audience to write their comments about the movie on cards. If the audience doesn't like the movie, the producer may decide to reedit or change certain parts.

If the producer and studio representative are happy with the film, they tell the laboratory to make many, sometimes hundreds, of prints of the film. These **release prints** will be "released," or sent to the theaters around the world that have arranged to show the movie.

## After the Movie Is Finished

The group of people who arrange for a film to be seen in theaters work for a **distributor**. The distributor makes arrangements with movie theaters, called **exhibitors**, to "exhibit," or show, movies. The distributor works in an office called a **film exchange** because over time, one film is exchanged for another. The distributor often handles many films at a time.

At the film exchange, the distributor's **bookers**, or salespeople, talk to the exhibitor's program booker about the various films available. Together they decide how much

In the movie business, a movie theater is referred to as an "exhibitor."

the exhibitor must pay to rent the movie—which they refer to as a "picture"—when it will play at the theater, and for how long. When the negotiations are completed, a release print is sent to the theater.

Although distribution is the last part of the filmmaking process, how the movie is distributed often determines whether it will be successful. In fact, many movies are never even distributed to theaters! Films that do not play in theaters are often released for sale or rent on videotape for use on cable TV, local TV, or home VCRs, however.

How the film is distributed—that is, its advertising campaign, the publicity and public relations efforts it gets, what cities are selected to screen the film, and how many theaters screen the film—depends, to a large extent, on whether the film is a studio production or an independent production.

Studio films, which are produced by major production companies like Amblin' Entertainment, Steven Spielberg's company, typically get more attention than independent

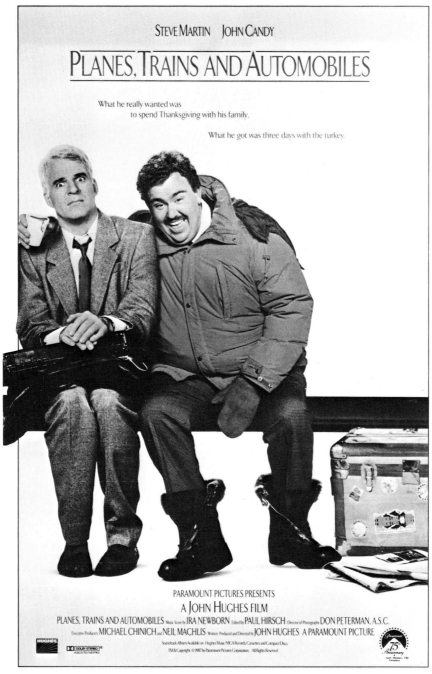

A movie poster is called a "one-sheet" in the film profession.

films. Distributors know that the studios will continue to provide them with new "product." Often distributors are more concerned about getting a constant supply of movies than they are about the quality of the movies.

### The Advertising Campaign

At the same time the bookers are arranging for the film to be shown, other people are busy developing the advertising campaign for the movie. The advertising people work with the producer and director to learn about the movie and how they think it should be presented to the public.

To plan the best strategy, advertising people consider many factors, such as the audience the movie is made for, the time of year the movie will be released, and the cities the movie will show in.

An important part of advertising a movie involves making previews, or **trailers**. Trailers for new movies are shown in theaters before the featured movie. Other ways movies are advertised include TV and radio commercials, newspaper and magazine advertisements, and billboards. Newspaper or billboard ads usually use a **production still** taken by the still photographer, a photographer who recorded all the important scenes of a film while it was being shot.

Some advertising material is prepared specially for the movie theaters that will exhibit the movie. These materials might include posters, called one-sheets, and cut-outs, life-sized cardboard displays of the stars of the movie.

Other experts create a promotional campaign for the movie. Public relations people, who specialize in creating the desire among the public to see the movie, plan ways to tell the public about the movie and the stars. They send press releases, brief stories about the stars and the making of the movie, to the media. They schedule media interviews for the stars and director.

If the movie's release is not in itself a major event, the public relations people may invent something to generate excitement about the movie. This is called "hype," which means "gimmicks designed to stimulate or enliven." The purpose of hype is to build interest in a film where there otherwise might not be any.

If, in the end, the public likes the movie and the advertising and public relations campaigns are successful, the movie will become the "talk of the town." But if the talk is bad, and few people like the film, no amount of advertising or "hype" can save it. If a movie continues to do good business at the box office, it is said to have "legs," and its chances of becoming a hit are very good.

# Careers in the Movies

If you love movies, you might like to learn more about jobs in the motion picture industry. Below is a list of selected movie industry organizations and publications, which you can write to for information, and a list of books about the movie industry.

## United States Organizations & Associations

The Academy of Motion Picture
  Arts & Sciences
8949 Wilshire Boulevard
Beverly Hills, CA 90211

American Cinema Editors (ACE)
2410 Beverly Boulevard
Los Angeles, CA 90057

The American Film Institute
Center For Advanced
  Film Studies
2021 North Western Avenue
Los Angeles, CA 90027

The American Society of
  Cinematographers
1782 North Orange Drive
Hollywood, CA 90028

Director's Guild of America, Inc.
110 West 57th Street
New York, NY 10019

International Sound Technicians
P.O. Box 1726
11331 Ventura Boulevard, 2nd Floor
Studio City, CA 91614

Make-Up Artists & Hair Stylists,
  Local 706
11519 Chandler Boulevard
North Hollywood, CA 91601

Motion Picture Costumers,
  Local 705
1427 North La Brea Avenue
Los Angeles, CA 90028

Motion Picture Editor's Guild
7715 Sunset Boulevard
Suite #220
Los Angeles, CA 90046

Motion Picture Lab Technicians
165 West 46th Street
New York, NY 10036

Producer's Guild of America
400 South Beverly Drive
Suite #11
Beverly Hills, CA 90212

Screen Actor's Guild (SAG)
7065 Hollywood Boulevard
Los Angeles, CA 90028

Screen Extra's Guild
3629 Cahuenga Boulevard West
Los Angeles, CA 90068

Stuntman's Association
4810 Whitsett Avenue
North Hollywood, CA 91607

Stuntwomen's Association
202 Vance Street
Pacific Palisades, CA 90272

Writer's Guild of America—East
555 West 57th Street
New York, NY 10019

Writer's Guild of America—West
8955 Beverly Boulevard
Los Angeles, CA 90048

## Canadian Organizations

The Association of Canadian Film
  Craftspeople
65 Heward
Toronto, Ontario M4M 2T5

Canadian Society of
  Cinematographers (CSC)
30 Niagara Street
Toronto, Ontario M6J 2L4

The Canadian Film Institute
150 Rideau Street
Ottawa, Ontario K1N 5X6

## Select Publications

*American Film*
6671 Sunset Boulevard
Suite #1514
Hollywood, CA 90028

*The Hollywood Reporter*
6715 Sunset Boulevard
Hollywood, CA 90028

*Daily Variety*
5700 Wilshire Boulevard
Suite #120
Los Angeles, CA 90036

*The Producer's Masterguide*
330 West 42nd Street
16th Floor
New York, NY 10036

# Books

Emmens, Carol A. *Stunt Work and Stunt People.* New York: Franklin Watts, 1982.

Gleasner, Diana C. *The Movies: Inventions That Changed Our Lives.* New York: Walker and Co., 1983.

Hutchison, David. *Film Magic: The Art and Science of Special Effects.* New York: Prentice Hall Press, 1987.

Ireland, Karin. *Hollywood Stuntpeople.* New York: Julian Messner, 1980.

London, Mel. *Getting Into Film.* Rev. ed. New York: Ballantine Books, 1985.

Mabery, D.L. *George Lucas.* Minneapolis: Lerner Publications, 1987.

———. *Steven Spielberg.* Minneapolis: Lerner Publications, 1986.

Pincus, Edward, and Steven Ascher. *The Filmmaker's Handbook.* New York: New American Library, 1984.

Thurman, Judith, and Jonathan David. *The Magic Lantern: How Movies Got to Move.* New York: Atheneum, 1978.

# Glossary

**animation:** photographing a series of drawings or objects in changing positions, one frame at a time. There are many different types of animation, for example **cel animation, claymation, hands-on animation,** and **puppet animation**.

**answer print:** the first print of a finished movie, sometimes also known as the trial print

**automatic dialogue replacement:** a technique whereby dialogue is recorded after a film has been shot and is used to replace the original sound recording of the actors' voices

**best boy:** the chief lighting electrician

**booker:** a person who works for a film distributor, negotiating movie rental fees and screening times with exhibitors (theaters)

**clap slate:** an identification sign that shows a movie's title, which scene is being shot, and other important information. It is held in front of the camera before each take begins, so that the shots can be identified easily later on.

**composite photography:** a special effect that combines separately photographed images onto one strip of film

**continuity:** matching of action from one take to another. For example, actors' clothes must remain exactly the same throughout a scene, even if it was filmed over several days and from many camera positions or angles.

**distributor:** a company, or a person, who arranges for films to be shown in movie theaters

**dolly:** a movable camera platform

**dubber:** a machine used to play music and sound effects in time with pictures

**exhibitor:** a movie theater

**film exchange:** a place where film distributors work, arranging the screening of many different movies

**first cut:** the first edited version of a movie

**format:** the shape and size of film, for example IMAX® or 35 mm

**frame:** one of a series of individual pictures that make up a film

**gaffer:** a lighting technician

**grip:** a crew member who carries equipment, such as lights, around a movie set

**grosses:** the amount of money taken in at theater box offices

**lead:** the main role in a movie

**light meter:** an instrument used to measure the amount of light falling on a set

**live action film:** film of real people and things, rather than animation

**mix:** the combining of sound effects, music, and actors' voices onto the movie sound track

**motion picture:** a series of still pictures that are projected onto a screen in rapid succession

**on location:** filming that takes place in the real world, not in a studio or specially designed set

**optical negative:** a photographic copy of a movie sound track

**period story:** a movie or story set in the past

**principal photography:** the filming of the main scenes of a movie

**production still:** a still photograph of a scene from a movie

**release print:** a copy of a film sent to exhibitors

**script notes:** detailed information about each scene of a movie

**shoot:** film or photography session

**shooting script:** the final version of a movie or television script, detailing the order in which the scenes should be shot and the dialogue to be spoken by the actors

**splicing block:** a special device that a film editor uses for taping together scenes of a film

**stand-ins:** people who look similar to the star actors in a film and who stand in their place while lighting is being checked before filming starts

**standing set:** a set that is used over and over again in different movies

**stock:** still photographic or movie film

**stop-motion photography:** a special effects technique in which one frame of film is exposed at a time, creating an illusion of movement

**story lines:** ideas for movies

**studio:** a motion picture company or a place where motion pictures are made

**take:** one uninterrupted scene of a movie

**theatrical film:** a feature film

**trades:** movie industry newspapers

**trailer:** a preview (usually three minutes long) of an upcoming movie

**treatment:** a brief statement about how ideas are to be presented on film

**work print:** the name given to the dailies once they are used for editing

# Index